DARE
TO
DREAM

Trusting God with the
Details

The Life of Joseph

Herbert Dickerson

~Dedication~

This book is dedicated to my father, Herbert Amos Dickerson who is resting in the arms of the Lord. I am thankful for my father who taught me many different things about life and living. To my mother, Shirley Ann Dickerson who is also resting in the arms of the Lord. After my father's death, she was both father and mother for her four boys. My mother's role in life was to keep us in church and learn about God. She was a praying woman of God and praised God everywhere she would go.

~Acknowledgments~

If I attempted to acknowledge all who contributes to the writing of this book in some way I would fail to mention someone's name.

In order, not to make that mistake, I will do my acknowledgements without openly mentioning names.

First, I want to acknowledge my family and friends, my colleagues in ministry, church staff, church members of Orange Grove Missionary Baptist Church and Vance Street Church.

Above all, I want to thank God, my Heavenly Father for giving me the Grace to complete this book.

TABLE OF CONTENTS

DREAM WHAT YOU WILL, BUT LEAVE THE DETAILS TO GOD!

-Rev. Herbert Dickerson

DREAMS ALWAYS OUTLIVE THE DREAMER!

-Anonymous

EVERY GREAT DREAM
BEGINS WITH A
DREAMER,
ALWAYS
REMEMBER;
YOU HAVE THE
STRENGTH,
THE PATIENCE, AND
PASSION
TO REACH
FOR THE STARS
TO CHANGE THE
WORLD

- Author Unknown

Introduction

God gives us dreams. God's dream for us is a seed waiting to blossom. "And it shall come to pass in the last days, says God, that I will pour out of My Spirit on all flesh; Your sons and your daughters shall prophesy, Your young men shall see visions, Your old men shall dream dreams. And on My menservants and on My maidservants I will pour out My Spirit in those days; And they shall prophesy. (Acts 2:17-18). Why does God give us dreams? He gives us dreams to encourage our hope. He gives us dreams so that we can pursue our purpose. He also gives us dreams so that His plan for our lives will be fulfilled.

There was a time in history when humankind did not have the Bible as we do today. The ancient followers of God did not have formal churches and ministers who preached and taught the Holy Scriptures. We might expect that during those periods in humankind's history with God-the primary source of communication was through a chosen spokesperson such as a prophet or Judge. But God also spoke clearly to His people through visions and dreams.

We may not think that such methods as visions and dreams are needed today- especially since we have God's Word, the Bible, in print. We know and believe that the Bible is the Word of God and it speaks directly to us, and provides wisdom, guidance and instruction for living a righteous life that is pleasing to God.

However, we can see from Acts 2:17-18 in the last days, God will increase His use of dreams and visions. This does not mean the Bible has less significance or that in any way dreams will replace the authority of the Word of God or the role it has in the life of a Christian.

Far from replacing the Bible, the purpose of God-given dreams (not all dreams come from God) is that we might envision living our lives according to the tenants of our faith just as described in the Bible.

The Bible teaches us that we can live our lives in a way that pleases God and the Holy Spirit's purpose is to implant that kind of dream in the heart of every person. It is my desire that every person who reads this book will determine to find God's will for their lives and never give up on their pursuit of the dreams that God has given them.

This book is a dedicated study of the Life of Joseph. Joseph's journey was like a roller coaster with many difficult twists and turns, but he was persistent in his pursuit of his God-given dream.

When we examine Joseph's story, we discover that his life was held together by one consistent thread- he had a dream. His dream from God that held him close to God. His dream was bigger than his circumstances. His dream was preparing him for a future that was not yet known. Joseph had an enormous dream and an enormous God to accompany it. All the circumstances said, "No Way" but God said, "No, this way."

Dreams are more than just your subconscious activities when you sleep – and they are more than your imagination or a distraction when you are awake.

So then, what is a dream? It is a condition or achievement that is longed for, an aspiration, an inspiring picture for the future that energizes your mind, will and emotions. It is a way for God to show you His plans and your purpose.

God-given dreams empower you to do everything you can to achieve them in spite of setbacks, delays, or people who don't believe in the dreams.

The American Heritage Dictionary tells us that dreams are a series of images, ideas and emotions occurring in certain stages of sleep. It also tells us that you don't have to be physically asleep to dream, and that dreams can occur as an involuntary vision while awake.

Dreams are the images of a future. They are the vision we hold of the future. Images that allows us to creatively see the possibilities even when we have not yet formulated the process for achieving the vision we hold of the future.

Dreams are also the engines of our lives and our ministries. These engines are supernaturally powered by God who is the architect of our dreams, and of the plans for our future.

Although there are other ways in which we can receive God's direction for our lives- dreams are a means for God to engage the human spirit (Numbers 12:6, Then He said,

"Hear now My words: If there is a prophet among you, *I*, the Lord, make Myself known to him in a vision; I speak to him in a dream. Joel 2:28, "And it shall come to pass afterward That I will pour out My Spirit on all flesh; Your sons and your daughters shall prophesy, Your old men shall dream dreams, Your young men shall see visions. Acts 2:17, 'And it shall come to pass in the last days, says God, That I will pour out of My Spirit on all flesh; Your sons and your daughters shall prophesy, Your young men shall see visions, Your old men shall dream dreams.

Why dreams? God gives us dreams which can be accomplished because they are the products of His desires, dreams that spring from His plans for our lives.

God places His dreams in those who will carry them out. Dreams provide a purpose for living. Without a purpose for living our lives can become drab and dull. Without a purpose for living, we live without promise and expectation.

God's purpose shapes your dreams and God's dreams shape your purpose. Pursuing God-given dreams is the cornerstone to discovering your divine purpose in life. Your dreams boldly answer the questions:

Why am I here? What is my purpose? What is God's Will for my life?

Today, I want to encourage you to dream. Be a Dreamer, and Dream Big. You can dream big because God is able to do exceedingly and abundantly above all that we can ask or dream according to God's power that works in us.

Ephesians 3:20 - Now to Him who is able to do exceedingly abundantly above all that we ask or think, according to the power that works in us.

You can dream big, because God has placed within our hearts the hopes and dreams that He wants to fulfill for us. So start dreaming, because dreams have their origin in where we are, and give insight into what we should be doing now to pursue them. Envision your efforts and allow your mind to see a future those efforts create.

God wants us to dream and dream big. To limit your dreams is to limit how you see God fulfilling His purpose and plan for you. Jeremiah 29:11 states, "For I know the thoughts that I think toward you, says the LORD, thoughts of peace, and not of evil, to give you an expected end."

If you have given up on your dreams, it's time to dream again. As a reminder, Proverbs 13:12 says, "Hope deferred makes the heart sick: but when the desire comes, it is a tree of life."

Dreams without effort or execution simply dies away with the dreamer. Never allow your God-given dreams to die. Dreams come to reality when the dream is cultivated and stimulated by the dreamer. Determination is important because every dream has its enemies, its opponents, and obstacles. Dreams and dreamers will encounter people who will cross-examine their dreams in the courtroom of life and public opinions. Dream Anyway!!

Dream of something Better, Bigger, and Greater for yourself.

Write down your Dreams. Set goals for your Dreams. Dream beyond where you are. Dream to where you Desire to be.

Lastly, Dream New, Fresh, and Dream Differently.

-Rev. Herbert Dickerson

EVERY DREAM HAS A RIGHT TO LIVE

-Dr. Kelley Varner

Chapter 1
Be a Dreamer –Dream BIG

In our introduction, we defined dreams as a condition or achievement that is longed for, an aspiration. A dream is an inspiring picture of the future that energizes your mind, your will and emotions, empowering you to do everything you can to achieve it regardless of the struggles and circumstances one must face.

The life of Joseph is an example for us to look at, to help us to realize how we can see all of our extra-ordinary dreams, hopes, and visions become a reality.

Romans 15:4, "For whatever was written in earlier times was written for our instructions so that through perseverance and the encouragement of the Scriptures we might have hope.

Joseph's story epically begins in Chapter 37 of the book of Genesis. Genesis begins with the narration of the story of creation, the fall of man, the flood of the earth, and the birth of the nation of Israel. Genesis chronicles the stories of the Patriarchs – Abraham, Isaac and Jacob.

Joseph's story is an example of God's divine intervention in the form of a dream. At its core are both a purpose and a plan. The purpose was to establish Joseph in a position of authority, so that he could preserve the promise made to

Abraham. The plan was to deliver Abraham's offspring so that they could fulfilled promise, and become the great nation that God had established.

Genesis 37: 1-5, Jacob lived in the land where his father had stayed, the land of Canaan. This is the account of Jacob's family line. Joseph, a young man of seventeen, was tending the flocks with his brothers, the sons of Bilhah and the sons of Zilpah, his father's wives, and he brought their father a bad report about them. Now Israel loved Joseph more than any of his other sons, because he had been born to him in his old age; and he made an ornate robe for him. When his brothers saw that their father loved him more than any of them, they hated him and could not speak a kind word to him. Joseph had a dream, and when he told it to his brothers, they hated him all the more.

God desires for us to dream big and any God-given dream is always larger than we can see and greater than we are.

Joseph according to Genesis 37:5 was a dreamer and He dreamed BIG. Dreaming Big meant that Joseph dreamed beyond his own imagination and greatness. His dream was a preview of a God ordained time when he would be intentionally positioned for God's purposes.

Joseph, one of the 12 sons of Jacob had a dream where he would rise up in authority over his brothers and they would bow down to him. He told his brothers about his dreams and from that point on, his life and his family's life was never the same. When you examine the lives of people who have changed the world, they were dreamers with Big dreams.

The capacity to dream was always the secret of those who brought about great change.

Dreams feed the soul and give wings to the intelligence and make a great difference in our existence.

Dreams have the ability to change our lives and affect change in the world.

Ben Franklin encouraged the other founding fathers to push for independence for the colonies after he had a dream. He was able to see beyond what was, to what could be, and foresee a future as an independent nation.

Albert Einstein theory of relativity was inspired by a dream.

Martin Luther King's, "I Have a Dream" speech was inspired from an actual dream. This moved him from the point of talking about it in his speech on the Washington Mall to a movement for equality and freedom for a nation.

Frederick August Kekule discovered the chemical structure benzene, one of the 20 most widely used chemicals in the United States, and he saw it first in a dream. He went on to say, "Let us learn to dream gentleman, and then we may perhaps find the truth."

It is in our dreams that God not only speak truth, but also where we can discover God's purpose for our lives.

Jeremiah 29:11 For I know the plans I have for you, says the LORD, They are plans for good and not for evil, to give you a future and hope. It is through dreams that we discover his plans and purpose for our lives.

When I was a young man, I dreamed often about things, places, and people that at times seemed familiar, and at other times were strange and unknown. When I reflect on this time in my life, some of my dreams I understood, but there were other times when my dreams didn't make sense to me. What was clear is that my dreams were a part of God's plan, and His purpose for my life. Those dreams often served as a compass for my journey.

One of the most memorable examples of a big dream occurred shortly after I finished seminary. As I was praying and asking God for a job, I realized that I was having the same dream. I remember having a repetitive and vivid dream of a waterfall, and I knew that the next place that God was taking me would be near it. Then it happened. I applied for a job at a large American company, and on the day of my interview - as I drove onto campus - there in front of me was a waterfall. I knew that this was the place that God had shown me in a dream.

Two days after the interview, I received a letter informing me that the company was not hiring at this time. Although confused, I asked God if I had misunderstood the dream He had given me. God answered in this way. In less than two hours, I received a call from the human resources department offering me the job and fulfilling a God-given dream.

Dreams don't just happen when we are asleep. Dreams can occur while we are awake. Dreams happen when we can imagine beyond our wildest dreams, when we choose to think outside the box, when we can throw off the constraints of the way things are and look beyond all of that to see the way things could be. Dreams happen when we take God out of the box.

We can safely say dreams are God's picture, God's vision or God's blueprint for a preferred future that helps us to fulfill our purpose in life.

Things weren't good for Joseph's family then God gives Joseph a dream – two dreams in fact. Genesis 37:5-9 Now Joseph had a dream, and he told *it* to his brothers; and they hated him even more. So he said to them, "Please hear this dream which I have dreamed: There we were, binding sheaves in the field. Then behold, my sheaf arose and also stood upright; and indeed your sheaves stood all around and bowed down to my sheaf." And his brothers said to him, "Shall you indeed reign over us? Or shall you indeed have dominion over us?" So they hated him even more for his dreams and for his words. Then he dreamed still another dream and told it to his brothers, and said, "Look, I have dreamed another dream. And this time, the sun, the moon, and the eleven stars bowed down to me.

At age 17, Joseph received his dreams from God and he was obviously naïve or just plain clueless because the way in which he talked about his dreams, caused his relationships with his brothers to go from bad to worse. The second dream he tells his father and is rebuked for what was perceived as self-elevation. Genesis 37: 9-11 Then he dreamed still another dream and told it to his brothers, and said, "Look, I have dreamed another dream. And this time, the sun, the moon, and the eleven stars bowed down to me." So he told *it* to his father and his brothers; and his father rebuked him and said to him, "What *is* this dream that you have dreamed? Shall your mother and I and your brothers indeed come to bow down to the earth before you?" And his brothers envied him, but his father kept the matter *in mind*.

Joseph was 30 when he stood before Pharaoh and began to enter into the fullness of his destiny. (Genesis 41:46) Joseph was thirty years old when he stood before Pharaoh king of

Egypt. And Joseph went out from the presence of Pharaoh, and went throughout all the land of Egypt.

From the age of 17 to 30 was 13 years period of equipping and training in the School of Life occurred for Joseph. This was when Joseph grew to know God. But it also teaches us that the fulfillment of our dreams doesn't come over night. Sometimes, God takes us through the school of life to prepare us not only for the fulfillment of the dream, but also to know Him.

Yes, God has a dream for each of us, a destiny, and a purpose. Many of us desire to know what it is – for our lives.

Our pursuit should be more than just wanting to know the dream, or destiny or purpose. Our pursuit should be a desire to know God the giver of the dream, God's destiny for the dreamer, and God's purpose for a dreamer's life. It is only when we grow to know God that our dreams can be fulfilled.

Take time to know the giver of the dream, the giver of the destiny, the giver of the purpose and only then will you know your purpose.

Get to know God and you will get to know the dreams He has for you. Psalm 103:7 says "He made known His ways to Moses His acts to the Sons of Israel."

I believe God wants us to dream and dream big. Why? Because He is a Big God who wants to manifest His Big Dreams in and through us.

John Maxwell, in his book, "Put Your Dream to The Test" says that "each of you has the capability to visualize a dream – one that is rewarding and beneficial – and most of you have the ability to accomplish it."

Maxwell highlights ten important questions you must answer to test your dream. I suggest that you only need to ask one – What is the Big Dream that God has given me?

WE CREATE
OUR
TOMORROW
BY WHAT WE
DREAM
TODAY
-Author Unknown

Chapter 2
What are Dreams made of?
(Genesis 37:1 – 50:10)

"If you don't know where you are going, you might wind up somewhere else." Yogi Berra

I believe every person have a dream placed in their heart. It is not the kind of dream like winning the lottery or a million-dollar sweepstake which is really the desire to escape our present circumstance.

I am talking about a vision deep down inside that speaks to the very soul of a person. The thing we were born to do that draws from our gifts and talents, appeals to our highest ideals, and sparks the feeling of destiny in our life, the dream that links us to the success of our journey between the lines of a time to be born and a time to die.

In Genesis 37, we read of a dreamer by the name of Joseph. His dream story spans from Genesis 37 to Genesis 50, which is the last chapter in the first book of the bible. Quite a dream, but are not dreamers filled with a dynamic vision. Look closely at Joseph's dream as we examine Genesis 37: 5-11, One night Joseph had a dream, and when he told his brothers about it, they hated him more than ever. "Listen to this dream," he said. "We were out in the field, tying up bundles of grain. Suddenly my bundle stood up, and your bundles all gathered around and bowed low before mine!"

⁸ His brothers responded, "So you think you will be our king, do you? Do you actually think you will reign over us?" And they hated him all the more because of his dreams and the way he talked about them. Soon Joseph had another dream, and again he told his brothers about it. "Listen, I have had another dream," he said. "The sun, moon, and eleven stars bowed low before me!" This time he told the dream to his father as well as to his brothers, but his father scolded him. "What kind of dream is that?" he asked. "Will your mother and I and your brothers actually come and bow to the ground before you?"**¹¹** But while his brothers were jealous of Joseph, his father wondered what the dreams meant.

We have the advantage of reading ahead to see the fulfillment of his dream. But the journey wasn't easy. No visionary will have an easy time moving across the dream terrain to the fulfillment state.

Joseph felt the jealousy of others, and in this case, it was his own brothers. Joseph was almost killed for the dream that he held in the depths of his heart. Even as he was being sold into slavery, he refused to let go of the dream. Although we think of dreams hoped for as being wonderful - this wasn't quite the picture for Joseph. Joseph, even became the object of seduction for the king's wife but he did not lose sight of the dream despite the difficulties that he endured. Joseph remained faithful to God and to the dream.

Look at some of the trials he went through for the sake of his dream. Joseph did not give into Potiphar's wife so he was falsely accused by her of attempted rape. Her word against his- the owner against the slave. We know without reading ahead who would win the battle.

Potiphar's response to the accusation was that he had him jailed. This should have been enough to end the dreamers vision of the future- but it did not end there.

In Joseph's case, the opposition worked as a refiner's fire in his life. Joseph was able to be used by God to interpret the dreams of others- cupbearer and a baker that directly served Pharaoh. This opened the door for interpreting Pharaoh's dream and eventually the fulfillment, in God's time, of his own dream.

The path of dreamers usually follows the same path or a similar path. Their dreams are not generally accepted or realized for some time, but it doesn't stop the dreamer.

Henry Ford had a dream that grew out of his interest in mechanical things as a young boy. He was intrigued by the automobile, and built his first one out in a shed behind his house.

His dream was to put the horseless carriage, at that time only available to the wealthy, into the hands of common people. His dream led him to be one of the founders of the Detroit Motor Company, where his fellow organizers balked at the idea of manufacturing their product inexpensively in order to sell to the masses.

Ford left the company, but did not leave his dream. In 1903, he organized the Ford Motor Company and produced the Model T. The first year only 6,000 cars were built, but only eight years later, over 500,000 cars a year rolled off the assembly line. They were able to reduce the cost from $850 to $360.00. Like Joseph, Ford's dream came to pass.

Let's look at what a dream will do.

1. **Dreams give us direction.**
   Have you ever known a person who doesn't have a clue about what they want in life, but are successful? Our dreams give us something worthwhile to aim at, it is a GPS or compass, telling us the direction to go. And if you move in any direction other than toward your dream, you will miss out on the opportunity necessary to be successful.

2. **Dreams increase your potential**.
   Without a dream, we may struggle to see the potential within ourselves because we are unable to

look beyond our current circumstances. Following our dreams, we begin to see ourselves in a new light. We are able to see ourselves as having greater potential and being capable of stretching and growing to reach our dreams. Like Joseph, every opportunity we meet, every resource we discover, every talent we develop, becomes a part of our potential to grow toward that dream.

3. **Dreams help us prioritize.**
It not only gives us hope for the future. A dream will add value to your work. It puts everything in perspective. Imagine if Joseph did not really believe his dream came from God. He probably would have made other choices with his life that would not have gotten him to where God intended him to be. But he realized that those things that came up along the journey, as unpleasant as they were, they would be used to ultimately contribute to the fulfillment of the dream.

Vince Lombardi said, "I firmly believe that any man's finest hour – his greatest fulfillment to all he holds dear – is that moment when he has worked his heart out in a good cause and laid exhausted on the field of battle – victorious." A dream provides the perspective that makes that kind of effort possible.

4. **Dreams give us a picture of the future.**
    Dreams gives us a mental picture in our mind, making us participants not spectators, so we are not blown by changing winds, but focused on what lies ahead, which increases our chances of success. I challenge you to dream big and act upon those dreams, in spite of problems, circumstances and obstacles.

5. **Dreams add value to life.**
    Dreams put everything into perspective. Imagine if Joseph had doubted that God could give him such grand dream, and questioned whether this dream was worth pursuing. He probably would have made different decisions, and the first may have been to remain silent and tell no one. But Joseph believed in his heart that this dream was the purpose for his life. and purpose provides value and value provides meaning to the relationship that we have with God, and that God has with us.

    Joseph may never have realized the fulfillment of the dream, if he had failed to believe that God had given it, and he should value it, because it was a gift of God. Joseph would not have gotten to where God intended him to be, if he had not recognized the value that the dream held for his future.

Here are six quick steps that will clear away the clutter and help you discover or fine-tune your dream.

1. Believe in your God-given dream and your ability to succeed. You cannot perform in a manner inconsistent from where you see yourself. The key word - perform.

2. Get rid of pride. People who are full of themselves usually don't have much room left over for a life – changing dream. Pride places the focus on appearance rather than potential and it prevents you from taking risks.

3. Cultivate constructive discontent. Discontent is a driving force that makes people search for their dreams. Complacency never brings success and only constructive discontent will motivate you to find your purpose and grow to reach your potential. Every invention registered in the U.S. Patent Office is the result of creative discontent. Each inventor, not satisfied with something the way it was, found a way to constructively overcome their dissatisfaction, either creating something new, or improving on what already existed.

4. Escape from habit – Habit can be defined as something you do without thinking. Habits can kill a dream because when you stop thinking, you stop

questioning and dreaming. You accept what is without considering what could be.

5. Balance creativity with character. Successful people have enough creativity to think it out and enough character to produce it with their hands. All the dreaming in the world will not work unless you wake up and go to work.

6. Invest in your dream emotionally. Your dream must go beyond your thoughts to your feelings. You must feel it Then after you feel it, you must seek after it. It takes hunger, tenacity and commitment to see a dream through to become a reality.

FOLLOW
YOUR HEART
&
YOUR DREAMS
WILL COME
TRUE

-Anonymous

Chapter 3

Dreams in the Midst of Dysfunction

Genesis 37:5 Now Joseph had a dream, and he told it to his brothers; and they hated him even more.

II Corinthians 4:7 But we have this treasure in earthen vessels, that the excellence of the power may be of God and not of us.

"God doesn't wait for us to get our act together before He gets involved in our lives."

Popular culture likes to portray dysfunctional families as endearing. Some examples of these portrayals may be the Connor family on the old television shows Roseanne Barr or the Bundy family on Married with Children.

Then there is the animated family we know as the Simpsons who are equally challenged. The father Homer has less than ideal parenting skills, Bart his son is the mischievous under-achiever, and his daughter Lisa is a neurotic vegetarian. The mother, Marge Simpson shows signs of deep-seeded depression. And Maggie, the baby of the family, has been sucking on a pacifier for 20 years.

All these television shows are nothing compared to the dysfunction of some of the families of the Bible.

For instance, in the beginning, the first family, Adam and Eve and their children had to deal with dysfunction ranging from deceitfulness, jealousy and murder. In the story of Jacob and Esau, there is the story of parental favoritism, deceit, deception, sibling rivalry and estrangement.

David, the writer of most of the book of Psalm, the man after God's own heart did not fare well with his wives and children. Instead, David who despite being a man after God's own heart, and a great King, managed to raise a world class dysfunctional family.

Even Jesus was raised in a dysfunctional family. He was not well liked by his brothers because of the societal backlash that came with their affiliation with Jesus and His ministry and message. (Matthew 13:54-58).

If we trace Biblical history, we notice that these and other dysfunctional families were the lineage of Jesus. Christ came through to be the Savior of the World.

Webster.com defines dysfunctional as abnormal or an unhealthy interpersonal behavior or interaction within a group.

Another definition of dysfunctional is a consequence of a social practice or behavioral pattern that undermines the stability of a social system. According to these definitions, I think it is safe to make a general diagnosis and all of us could agree that Joseph's family was dysfunctional – just like ours.

Joseph's father-Jacob was a "trickster" (I call him an opportunist) and his name literally means "deceiver". This started the day he was born. He and Esau were twins. When they were born, Esau was first, but Jacob was a close second, emerging with his hand on his brother's heel. Jacob's tricks did not stop there. He took advantage of Esau's hunger providing him with a warm meal in exchange for his birthright-which Esau agreed to give up. Then there was the time he obeyed his mother and tricked his blind, nearly dead father into blessing him with the patriarchal (death bed) blessing, which put him on the run. When Esau realized what had happened, he set out to kill Jacob. Therefore, Jacob was a con-man, running for his life when he met the love of his life: Rachel. The only problem was that Rachel's father Laban was a crafter than Jacob. He out conned the con man. With a promise from Laban to give him Rachel to wed, Jacob agreed to work seven years for Laban. After Jacob worked the seven years, Laban gave him a veiled bride who was his oldest daughter Leah instead to wed and only after the wedding night did Jacob realize what Laban had done. This cost Jacob another seven years of work just to get the one he wanted to begin with: Rachel.

Not only was Joseph's Father a trickster, but his mother was a lying, thieving, idolatress. The day Jacob left Laban; she stole an idol from her father's tent. When her father came looking for it, she lied and said she was having her period, so she would not have to get up. She had the idol hidden in the ground under her.

Talk about dysfunction family. Joseph had one- a textbook, characterized dysfunctional family. He had a trickster for a father, and an idolatress for a mother, not to mention ten brothers all of whom hated him. His father was married to a woman he did not love – Leah. Although Leah had given him four sons: Reuben, Simeon, Levi and Judah. Then there was Rachel the wife who he favored and loved. Rachel in her zealousness gave her maid – Bilhah to Jacob in an attempt to have children through her, because Rachel was barren. She had two sons by him: Dan and Naphtali. Then Leah, not wanting to be outdone by her younger, prettier sister, gave her maid-Zilpah to Jacob to have children through her as well. She had two sons also: Gad and Asher. All the contentiousness and sibling rivalry between these two sisters further perpetuated the family dysfunction. Jacob continued to be manipulated as the prize for each of them, one night as part of a bargain between Rachel and Leah. Leah wins the right to sleep with Jacob and had two more sons: Issachar and Zebulun. Finally, after praying to God for a son, Rachel the love of Jacob's life conceived. She gave him two sons: Joseph and Benjamin. As if her purpose was finally complete; Rachel the love of Jacob's life died while giving birth to Benjamin.

Not only did he have a dysfunctional family, but he spent the early life in a family of ten brothers that hated him. He had a step-mom, who realized that her husband loved his mother more than her, and on top of all that, his mother died. Growing up with a mother's love was not to be. Instead, Joseph endured jealousy daily. He had to endure being chosen as the father's favorite, which only fueled the anger of his brothers even more.

We tend to think of dysfunctional families as a problem unique to modern life, but Joseph's shows you otherwise. People have always been people. Human relationships have always been complicated by the sin nature all of us bear.

Joseph was born into a family whose complications rival those of many families today – including a stepmother, three sets of half-brothers and the loss of his mother.

It was a tangle of divided loyalties and resentments. Joseph could have easily become a victim of these circumstances, but he was learning that God was bigger than any circumstance.

In Genesis 37:4 when the brothers saw that their father loved Joseph more than any of them, they hated him and could not speak a kind word to him and God's response to his brother is in Genesis 37:5, Joseph had a God-given dream and when he told it to his brothers, they hated him all the more.

Our story starts in Genesis 37:2 when Joseph was 17 years old, he was tending sheep with his older brothers, the sons of Jacob's two concubines. He was already in the middle of a dysfunctional family. So often we don't create our own dysfunctions, we just find ourselves in the middle of them.

I believe that the family is a microcosm of society and what we observe in the family is a little picture of the big picture. If something exists in the family, it exists in our world and in our churches.

It's good to know that the Word of God speaks into our dysfunction. The world says just get over it, but the Word of God says I know where you are, what you are in, but I can still use you and get you out of it, if you follow me.

The main problem with our dysfunction is that seldom do we recognize that we are dysfunctional.

Joseph's father, Jacob, whose name is changed to Israel by God clearly shows favoritism in the family. Joseph received a special coat while the other brothers did not. The Bible describes it as Joseph's coat of many colors.

Favoritism was what Jacob, Joseph's father, grew up with. Remember his mother Rebecca favored him while his dad Isaac favored his brother Esau, and they were at war with each other fighting over whose favorite child was supposed to get the inheritance.

Favoritism breeds hatred. But hatred was also normal in the family. Jacob had two wives. He loved Rachel, but tolerated Leah! The attitude shown will be the attitude replicated.

We often assume that our private sins hurt no one but ourselves. But sins of character have a way of touching everyone with whom we have contact especially those we love in our family.

You would think with all this dysfunction, Joseph would not have a choice, even his great-grandfather, Abraham, and great-grandmother, Sarah, had some dysfunctions. But God gives Joseph a God-given dream in the midst of all this dysfunction.

Notice the division among the family. Each member chose sides causing the family to be at odds with one another. But as desperate and divided as things are in this family, a dream is given, a seed is planted, hope is given that would change and entice nations and save the lives of his family and that dream is given to Joseph.

One may have been wondering with all that is going on in this family whether anything good could come out of all this. If our attention becomes fixated on the problems that they had and how wrong things are between the family members, we miss the point.

What's the point? God doesn't wait for us to get our act together. God doesn't wait for us to get our relationships straightened out before he begins working in and through us. And the evidence of this is that God gave Joseph a dream and his dream was a game changer.

To a family that is filled with hatred, bitterness, dysfunction, and division, God speaks and speaks through dreams. The dream is given to Joseph and it's not hard to get to the point of the dream. What Joseph sees in the dream is his brothers bowing and submitting to him.

The dream is given specifically to Joseph and we must ask what is God up to, how is God going to unfold and accomplish His plans in and through Joseph? God then decides one dream is not enough, He then gives Joseph a second dream, which really makes the same point as the first- there will be a time of submitting to God in repentance and obedience. In the midst of all this dysfunction God gives two dreams to Joseph- dreams that provides hope and purpose for the future.

Again, God doesn't wait for us to get our act together before He gets involved in our lives. If you notice, God chooses to work with people who are broken, confused and mixed up. Paul said it best in his second letter to the Corinthian church. Paul talks about the call of God. He states that God calls or chooses to use and work through broken, fragile, weary human beings.

He says it this way: We have this treasure in jars of clay to show that this all-surpassing power is from God and not from us (2 Corinthians 4:7).

Therefore, when you find yourself in the midst of the dysfunctional world, the dysfunctional family and yes even the dysfunctional church; don't allow yourself to get used to the status quo of dysfunction around you. God will not be content to leave you there because He has something better in mind. He calls us beyond the dysfunction, and instills a vision and a dream so that you can know Him.

Lessons Learned from a Dysfunctional Family

1. Dysfunction need not define who we are and who we become.

Between Genesis 37 and Chapter 50 a great deal takes place in Joseph's life. He suffers greatly because of the decisions of his brothers and what their betrayal did to him. However, he also manages by the grace of God, to rise from being a shepherd boy, from being a lowly house slave to a powerful ruler in Egypt. Joseph goes from a pit, to a prison and from a prison to a palace. As divided as Joseph's family was, a dream is given, a seed is planted and a God-give dream establishes his purpose.

Joseph's family life had some tumultuous relationships. And when we see the dysfunction, hatred and the contempt that comes between these brothers, you may feel like despairing over whether anything good could have come from this crazy collection of family members. But if our attention becomes fixated on the problems that they have, and how wrong things are between members, we miss the point.

The point is simple: God doesn't wait for us to get our act together. God doesn't wait for us to get our relationships straightened out before He begins working in and through us. And the evidence of this is that in the midst of this family dysfunction God gives Joseph a dream, while there was still hatred and jealousy. It's a big dream, a God-given dream. To a family that is filled with hatred, division and dysfunction to this family God speaks.

2. You need to break the cycle of dysfunction.

We all had some dysfunctional sins in our lives one way or another, most of the time we don't even know it because everyone else's family seems to be living the same way. But once God helps us to know right from wrong and gives us a dream, and we follow the dream, we will need to break the cycle of dysfunction.

Finally, the day came when Joseph had the opportunity to give back some of the mistreatment that his brothers had given to him. He chose not to and instead he forgave. Genesis 50:19-20 Joseph said to them, "Do not be afraid, for am I in the place of God? But as for you, you meant evil against me; but God meant it for good, in order to bring it about as it is this day, to save many people alive.

If he would have retaliated, then he would have continued the cycle of dysfunction. But Joseph breaks the cycle by forgiving his brothers of their wrongs. All the elements were in place for Joseph to continue the cycle of bitterness but he chose not to.

Joseph breaks the cycle of his dysfunctional family. He tells his brothers at the end don't be afraid. Joseph let's his brothers know he will treat them well. Joseph chose to change his family's dysfunction to fully functioning.

3. **You need to trust God in His dream for you and see a future of deliverance.**

Many of you might also come from a severe dysfunctional background like that of Joseph. No matter where you have come from never take on a victim's mentality. This creates a mindset of disability that helps you to come up with excuses. Excuses like, " they don't like me" or "my father did this" or "my mother was like this" But knowing where you are going by focusing on the goals and dreams God has given you, and by focusing on what God wants you to be- then you will make the changes you need to make- to get you where God intents for you to be.

God knows the dysfunctional background you have been in, but God has given you a dream that will bring greater in your life from now on.

IT'S BETTER TO HAVE AN IMPOSSIBLE DREAM THAN TO HAVE NO DREAM AT ALL.

-Anonymous

Chapter 4

Watch out for Dream Killers

Genesis 37:23-24 So it came to pass, when Joseph had come to his brothers, that they stripped Joseph of his tunic, the tunic of many colors that was on him. Then they took him and cast him into a pit. And the pit was empty; there was no water in it.

Jesus states in John 10:10 that the thief's desire is to steal, kill and destroy your life. And to counter that, Jesus says that he has come to give life in abundance. If you define the word abundance, it means beyond measure to have an advantage, to be rich, and overflowing. Whenever the enemy knows that God has a plan for His children, whenever he knows that God has a blessing for you, he will try to step in and intercept what is coming your way. The enemy does not want to see you living in abundance, he doesn't want to see you walking in your destiny, walking in your purpose, walking in your calling, or walking in your God-given dreams.

So, the enemy comes to steal and kill your inheritance and destroy your faith in God and your God-given dream.

Many times, we think that the thief comes to steal from us tangible things. The tangibles are those things that we can feel and we can see. Also, many times when we think that the enemy comes to kill our body and put sickness upon us.

But let's go a little deeper. Yes, all those things are true. The Devil comes to take all that he can and more. He comes to destroy our health, and our wealth, but he also comes to destroy our passions, desires and God-given dreams- but when He comes to destroy everything- he comes not just for things but for the relationship you have as a child of God.

In Genesis 37:5, Joseph had a dream but it was not just any dream, it was a God-given dream. God's dreams for our lives are always bigger than our dreams. Joseph was given a God dream and was excited so he told his family. Instead of family celebration, there was a plot to kill the dreamer and the dream.

God-given dreams will bring about rejection. Joseph was excited, but found that others were not so enthusiastic about his dream because of the vision he shared regarding their future.

So many people fail at this point. As soon as there is rejection, as soon as their God-given dream becomes unpopular to people they discard the dream, Joseph's brothers not only hated him, but hated his God dream as well.

The enemy doesn't step in just because you have a dream. The enemy tries to destroy you as soon as you decide to live out that dream. When you plan to live out your dreams the enemy steps in and attempts to destroy you. When you make up in your mind that you're going to walk in your dreams, desires, and the vision that God has given you, that is when the enemy looks to see who he may devour, what dreams he may devour.

Joseph brothers already disliked him because he was his father's favorite son. His father showed favoritism when he made him a coat of many colors-and although this increased his brothers disdain for him. It was not until Joseph had a dream that the enemy thought he must destroy him. The enemy used those who were close to Joseph to try and destroy him- and will use those who are close to you to try and destroy you and your God-given dream.

Watch out for dream killers. When you begin to walk in the dreams and the visions that God has given you- you will be plotting a course of success.

When you make up your mind that you are going to live out your God-given dreams be prepared for the flood of attacks from enemy. Isaiah 59:19 So shall they fear the name of the Lord from the west, And His glory from the rising of the sun; When the enemy comes in like a flood The Spirit of the Lord will lift up a standard against him. Never allow the enemy to stop you from dreaming and walking in your God given dreams. Never allow his attacks to deter you. Never allow the dream killers to be the voice of your dream. Never allow anything and anyone's unbelief to keep you from your belief that God-given you a dream that has meaningful purpose for your life.

His brothers made the statement, here comes the dreamer. People you think you can trust with your vision, people you think you can trust with your dreams, and you hope they will be there to support you- those are the ones that the devil will use to destroy your dreams.

Everything could be fine in your relationship with a brother, spouse, sister, close relatives, yes even a church member. Then, all of a sudden they turn left. Things begin to fall apart. The devil will use the ones that are closest to you. The people you thought should support you, and he uses them to distract you. So, he can kill your dreams, future, desires and ambitions.

Watch out for dream killers. Watch out for those who oppose you when God has called you to do something. Through eyes of doubt, disbelief and envy, they cannot see your dream as being possible. This may create a problem. Therefore, you must watch out for dream killers. Be careful with whom you share your ambition and dreams.

Dream killers are those who cannot or refuse to see or invest in your vision. They are those who envy and will try to kill you in the process. They are those who have multiple excuses of why you cannot or will not do what God has called you to do. Like Joseph's brothers, they may use excuses like you are too young; some may even think you are too old dependent on your current status. They are those who question your ability and education saying that you are not smart enough or you don't have the adequate resources. Whatever the case, watch out for dream killers!

The enemy's desire is to stop you from progressing. If you are not doing the will of God, you cannot express to others what God may have for you. If you are not living your dreams, you may have to faced some dream killers somewhere down the line.

The devil has spiritually killed some of us. Even though we are physically still here. Going through the motions of life. But if you are not living the dream that God has given you, you are not really living. Some of you had a dream of starting your own business, but somebody told you that you could not succeed.

Some had dreams of finishing college, but some obstacles blocked your way. God is calling you to a higher calling, but the enemy, (not God) is telling you that you're not qualified. The list could go on and on, but please watch out for those Dream Killers.

Be attentive to your dreams. Because God talks to us in our dreams. The Bible tells us in Job 33:4, "The Spirit of God has made me; and the breath of the Almighty gives me life."

Whether we are sleeping or resting, God is opening up our ears to the vision that He sees for us. It is time to wake up from your dreams, and wake up from the vision because as long as we are asleep, we cannot live out Dream.

Wake up! The alarm clock is going off. Get up and walk in your vision and walk in your dreams! Get away from the dream killers.

REMEMBER:

Every dreamer will deal with haters.

Every dreamer will have naysayers.

Everyone will not believe in your dreams.

Everyone will not support your dreams.

Everyone will not embrace your dreams.

Some people will try to kill your dreams.

Everyone will not be happy about your dreams.

TO ACCOMPLISH GREAT
THINGS,
YOU MUST NOT ONLY
ACT,
BUT ALSO DREAM;
NOT ONLY
PLAN,
BUT ALSO
BELIEVE

-Anatole France

Chapter 5
Don't allow your Dreams to die in the Process

Genesis 37:23-24 So it came to pass, when Joseph had come to his brothers, that they stripped Joseph of his tunic, the tunic of many colors that was on him. Then they took him and cast him into a pit. And the pit was empty; there was no water in it.

There is something to be said for those who do not give up easily on things and prevail in persistence with prayer, faith and hope. Napoleon Hills says, "One of the most common causes of failure is the habit of quitting when one is overtaken by temporary defeat."

Any dream worth pursuing is going to experience roadblocks and setbacks along the way, but that is no reason to stop pursuing the dream. Don't allow your dreams to die in the Pit.

Let's look at some of the challenges that a dreamer may go through, but if they are willing to stick it out- then the dream will be fulfilled or come true. dreams will come true. Look at the life of a dreamer.

Joseph was thrown into the pit. Why does God allow us or permit us to have pit experiences even when it's a God-given dream? Contrary to what some may say the child of God does have pit experiences even while pursuing their God-given dreams. God never shelters us to the degree that he does not permit us to go through some experiences. If we don't bear our cross while pursuing our dreams, we will never wear a crown. I believe that the life of Joseph gives us clues as to why God permits us to be thrown into a pit.

God always has reasons for your pit experiences. What then are the processes of our pit experiences?

When looking at the circumstances of Joseph's life it appears each negative event produced another negative. Thankfully when we survey the totality of Joseph's life we can attest that the end result was a positive result.

Charles Caleb Colton in his book, "Overcoming Adversity", makes this statement, "all adverse and depressing influences can be overcome, not by fighting, but by rising above them." Look at the negative that takes place in Joseph's life:

1. If Joseph's brothers had not sold him to the Midianites, then he never would have gone to Egypt.
2. If he had never gone to Egypt, he would have never been sold to Potiphar.
3. If he was never sold to Potiphar, Potiphar's wife would have never accused him of rape.

4. If Joseph was never accused of rape, then he would have never gone to prison.
5. If he was never put in prison, he would have never met the baker and butler of Pharaoh.
6. If he had never met the baker and butler, he never would have interpreted their dreams.
7. If he had never interpreted their dreams, he would have never been able to interpret Pharaoh dreams.
8. If he had never interpreted Pharaoh dreams, he would have never been made prime minister.
9. If he had never been made prime minister he would never been able to wisely administrate for the severe famine coming upon the region.
10. If the family in Canaan would have died from the famine, then his family would have died in Canaan.
11. If the family in Canaan would have died from the famine, Jesus the Messiah could not come forth.
12. If the Messiah could not come forth, then Jesus would not have come.
13. If Jesus would not have come, we would die in our sins and without hope.

Notice all these negatives where a part of the process that started with a God-given dream and a Pit. The definition of a process is a systematic series of actions directed to something, and the process that a product or person goes through determines the quality of the product.

Joseph went through a process to become the man God desired for him to be and to see his dreams come true. Most of us at one time or another have had a dream to do something big for God, but what can happen is our dreams can be put to sleep or died in the middle of the process.

Never allow the process to steal your dream or to die in the pit. A pit is a place of darkness, isolation and loneliness yet because of Joseph's God-given dream, God allowed him to be put in a pit and survive. Why?

As human beings, we so often look at or tend to focus on the negative as if the negative tells the whole story. The pit to us seems to be a negative, but if it was not for the negative God could not show off his powers like he does.

If it wasn't for the negative situation in life- God could not show up in the middle of your situation and blow everybody's mind with His awesome power. He could not turn the negative into a positive like He does- just for the benefit of believers and unbelievers alike.

In order to understand the negative, we must first understand the darkness. The pit was a place of darkness. Darkness is the image and appearance of everything negative. Dark is an opportunist seizing every moment that is available.

Darkness is a very dominant force to be reckoned with, yet Joseph finds himself in darkness. If we go back and look, it

51

was in a negative situation where the Bible begins recording. The story of creation begins with a negative.

The very first recorded act of God was in darkness, "In the beginning, God created the heavens and the earth." (Genesis 1:1).

Why? Because what He was working on wasn't ready for the light – Joseph even with his God-given dream wasn't ready yet for the light.

If we would remember before there were digital cameras, film was developed in what we called a dark room. While attending community college, one of my electives was how to use a camera and develop pictures in a dark room.

As we take a picture, there is a very quick yet small burst of light onto the roll of film. This image is burned into the film and it waits to go through the process of development. The process of development must be taken in an environment that will ensure that the image will be preserved.

All necessary measures must be taken to protect the image from premature light. The piece of film that goes through the process of the dark room is called a negative. After it has gone through solvents and solutions, after the fan and the drying has taken place and now the negative has light applied to it, then the positive image begins to come forth.

Something that was preserved by the darkness. Something that was there all along, you could not see it.

Don't let your dreams die in the darkness of the pit, it is there that God is developing you. He sees what you are not and He wants to make you what you could be. So, don't fight the pit. Even though the pit is full of negatives, it can only produce the positive.

Joseph finds himself in a pit, a pit that he was placed in by his brothers. But the same brothers that sent him down into the pit were the same ones that lifted him out of the pit. God could not leave Joseph in the pit, Joseph's destiny – His God-given dream wasn't in the pit!

But what was in the pit was a covenant between God, Abraham, Isaac and Jacob. What was in the pit was the future of his brothers, the future of a nation, the future of the church. God could not leave Joseph in the pit.

Why does God permit us to have pit experiences with our God-given dreams? Let me suggest to you that there are three lessons to be learned in the pit.

Lesson 1: A Pit experience teaches us to be patient.

Often God cannot do what he wants through us or in us because we are too impatient. Even with a God-given big dream, we must learn to be patient. Joseph needed to know that yes God gave him those dreams- but he would need to wait at least 13 years for them to come to culmination. If we are to see our dreams come to culmination, then we must learn how to walk in the darkness of our pits before we can shine in the light. The pit was God's way of positioning Joseph for what He had for him. God has to position us in the lowest point (pit) of our lives in order to elevate us to higher dimensions.

Lesson 2: The pit was Joseph's path to the Palace.

When God gives us dreams, we must understand that God has certain paths in which he wants us to go. The pits of life forces us to travel the way of the Lord and not our own way. God's way is always the best way.

Lesson 3: Joseph was not ready for what the Lord would have him to do.

Joseph needed to be prepared. He needed to be prepared. Notice that Joseph's first step toward the palace was a pit. Don't despise the pit. And don't dismiss the pit as being invaluable. It is the place where God is developing you for the dream that will provide you with a God-given purpose for your life. The pit is the preparation for the fulfillment of the big dream and your first step towards the palace. Embrace your seasons of darkness. God was with Joseph the entire time, and God is willing to remain with you from your Pit to the divine palace for your life.

Chapter 6

Trusting God with the Details

Genesis 50:19-21 Joseph said to them, "Do not be afraid, for am I in the place of God? [20] But as for you, you meant evil against me; but God meant it for good, in order to bring it about as it is this day, to save many people alive. [21] Now therefore, do not be afraid; I will provide for you and your little ones." And he comforted them and spoke kindly to them.

Pursue your dreams and you will be amazed about what God can achieve in your life. Joseph's life was anything but peaceful. He was sold into slavery by jealous brothers, thrown into prison on false charges. Yet, he remained free of bitterness or regret.

God acts as the great architect behind the worst of circumstances and during a final confrontation with his brothers, Joseph makes a great theological truth. "What others intend to harm us, God can orchestrate for our benefit."

We don't know and realize how beautifully God is working in our lives until our dreams come to pass.
We don't know and realize how God is working until His plan is zoomed in and we see it for what it is. We spend our years, months, and days waiting on God often anxiously for Him to reveal what He is doing.

In these times, we must trust God with the details of our lives and the dreams God has given us. Not only must we trust God with the details of our lives and dreams, but we must trust that God is working in the midst of our circumstances to bring about His goodwill for us. One of the classics examples of this is Joseph. His dream caused him to go through pain, betrayal, trials, triumph and prosperity. In the mist of it all, he looked to God and trust His sovereign purpose.

When we walk in our God-given dreams, we must be able to handle the set up and endure the pits and prisons of life. If we can endure the pressure, we will emerge as Joseph did with our faith, character and loyalty to God intact.

Our God-given dreams sometimes come with the cost the same way. There is a cost at the toll roads are toll bridges in our nature and our natural world there are tolls to be paid in walking into our dreams. There is a cost to cross over into the greatness of your God-given dream, unlike the toll bridges that collect money, the toll that one pays for dreaming is sometimes paid by our painful moments or disappointments, our sleepless nights and cloudy days.

We must be willing to pay the costs and realize that God is collecting our fee for the greatness He placed inside of us. Our God-given dreams are designed to bring God's glory to Him and bless us at the same time.

What we must remember is that we have an adversary who knows this therefore; what God meant for good our adversary means it for our bad. When we trust God with the details of our dreams, there is a doctrine that helps us understand how God handles the details of our dreams. Many times, God shows us only small parts of the dream, but never all the details.

The Doctrine that helps us is called Providence. Although this may not answer every question at least it provides the only possible basis for understanding. It is the doctrine of the providence of God.

In English the word, providence has two parts it's pro and video put together literally means to see before the word providence itself is not found in most modern translations of the Bible, but the concept is biblical. Providence refers to God's gracious oversight of the universe. Each of these words is important. God's providence is one aspect of His grace. Oversight means that He directs the course of affairs. The word universe tells us that God not only knows the big picture, but He also concerns himself with the smallest of details.

Joseph, in his dreams saw the ending of the dream. He saw himself in a place of authority and his brothers bowing down to him. Only God had the details of how Joseph would get to the place God had purpose for him. Providence is the invisible hand of God at work.

Here are five powerful statements that unfold the meaning of God's providence in more detail:

1. God upholds all things.

2. God governs all events.

3. God directs everything to its appointed end.

4. God does this all the time and in every circumstance.

5. God always does it for His glory.

The doctrine of God's providence teaches us several important truths.

First, God cares about the tiniest details of life. Nothing escapes His notice for He is concerned about the small as well as the big. In fact, with God there is no big or small. God knows when a sparrow falls and He know the numbers of hairs on our heads. He keeps track of the stars in the sky and the rivers that flows to the ocean. He sets the day of your birth and death. God ordains everything that comes to pass and in between.

Secondly, God uses everything and waste nothing. There are no accidents with God, only incidents. This includes events that seem to be the simplest, senseless tragedies.
 Thirdly, God's ultimate purpose is to shape His children into the image of Jesus Christ. He often uses difficult moments and human tragedies to accomplish that purpose.

Romans 8:29 For whom He foreknew, He also predestined *to be* conformed to the image of His Son, that He might be the firstborn among many brethren.

Many verses in the Bible teaches us these Truths:

- Acts 17:28
- Colossians 1:17
- Hebrews 1:3
- Proverbs 16:19
- Psalm 115:3

The doctrine of God's providence is a combination four other attributes.

Sovereignty- God is all powerful and in control.

Predestination- God is in charge of how the plan unfolds.

Wisdom- He makes no mistakes.

Goodness- God has our best interests at heart.

We should think of providence as the invisible visible hand of God moving through the circumstances of our lives.

With providence as our background, we will consider the dream of Joseph one final time because he was the favored son of his father Jacob. Favor doesn't always mean you are treated right. Joseph was the favored son, but he became the object of envy by his many brothers.

His brothers conspired to sell him to the Midianites who was passing by. They splashed his coat of many colors with the blood of a goat in order to make it appear that he had been killed by a wild animal. His brothers showed the coat to Jacob, who believe what his Sons told him and concluded that Joseph was dead. Joseph was taken to Egypt and there he was sold again to Potiphar who was over the federal security team.

In Genesis 39 we see that Joseph gain favor with Potiphar because the Lord was with him to bless him. Eventually Potiphar put Joseph in charge of his entire household, what a high honor for a Hebrew slave! Look what Favor will do.

Joseph was competent, confident, and good-looking. Potiphar's wife approached him about having a sexual affair. He refused and she persisted to the point when everyone else was gone she attempted to pull him down to her bed. Joseph fled from the scene leaving his cloak behind, humiliated by his refusal she accused him of rape. Though it was a false charge, Potiphar believed his wife and had Joseph put in prison.

~Remember God's Providence is Unfolding~

In prison Joseph prospered once again and gained the respect of his fellow prisoners and the guards. Why? Because the Lord was with him to bless him. Eventually, the cupbearer and the Baker were thrown in the same prison and Joseph befriended them. One night they both had dreams they could not interpret, but Joseph was able to interpret them with the Lord's help.

God will make room for your Gifts!

The dreams came true exactly as Joseph had predicted, the Baker was home, but the cupbearer was released. Joseph asked him to remember him after he was out, but he did not remember.

Two years passed and Pharaoh had a dream that he could not interpret. Then the cupbearer remembered Joseph amazing ability to interpret the dreams. He mentioned it to Pharaoh who ordered Joseph to be brought before him. Joseph correctly interprets his dreams and was rewarded by Pharaoh who made Joseph the Prime Minister of Egypt; a Hebrew slave becomes prime minister.

From the Pit to the Palace

Eventually a famine settled on the near east Jacob told his sons to go to Egypt and to buy some grain. In the process, of going, they met Joseph, the one they sold into slavery. They didn't realize it was their brother. This happened twice, then Joseph revealed his true identity. The brothers were in shock because they betrayed him, and now he is in position to get even. But Joseph doesn't, Joseph speaks the word. Genesis 45:5-8 But now, do not therefore be grieved or angry with yourselves because you sold me here; for God sent me before you to preserve life. For these two years the famine has been in the land, and there are still five years in which there will be neither plowing nor harvesting. And God sent me before you to preserve a posterity for you in the earth, and to save your lives by a great deliverance. So now it was not you who sent me here, but God; and He has made me a father to Pharaoh, and lord of all his house, and a ruler throughout all the land of Egypt.

But that's not the end of the story.

The brothers go back to Canaan and tell their father who is well in age now, that Joseph is still alive. Eventually, Jacob believe his sons, and makes the trip back with them to Egypt. He meets Joseph the son who he thought was dead for many years. Then Jacob meets Pharaoh who offers to let Joseph family settled in Egypt and they lived in peace for many years. Finally, Jacob dies at the age of 147.

Now it's just Joseph and his brothers, Joseph brothers now fear that because their father is dead that Joseph will be free to take revenge on them. They told Joseph that" before dad died, he told us to tell you to treat us kindly." One more deception to cover their guilt. But listen to Joseph's response the one who believes in the providence of God.

Genesis 50:19-20 Joseph said to them, "Do not be afraid, for am I in the place of God? But as for you, you meant evil against me; but God meant it for good, in order to bring it about as it is this day, to save many people alive.

How could Joseph talk like that after all that happened to him. The answer is simple, he saw God everywhere. Look how Joseph says it you meant evil against me, but God meant it for good. Both sides of the statement are true. What the brothers had done was indeed evil, and Joseph don't deny it. They are hundred percent responsible for their sin. God meant it for good, this statement doesn't mean that evil is not evil. It just means that God is able to take the evil actions of sinful men and use them to accomplish His plan.

Joseph saw the invisible hand of God at work in his life. Joseph understood that behind conniving brothers stood the Lord God who had orchestrated the entire affair in order to get him to the right place at the right time.

Joseph declared that though your motives were bad, God's motives were good. Although it took years and years for God's purpose to be clear, in the end Joseph saw the hand of God behind everything that had happened to him. Joseph dream came true. Dreams do come true.

Think about this. At just the right moment his brothers threw him in the pit. The Midianites came along, he was sold to Potiphar, then Potiphar's wife falsely accuse him. he meets the Baker and the cupbearer. The cupbearer remembers Joseph. Pharaoh called for Joseph to interpret the dreams, then Joseph was promoted from Prime Minister. Jacob sends his sons to Egypt. Joseph's family moves to Egypt. Pharaoh offers them the land of Goshen they settled there and prospered. All this happened and just a right moment and in the right way so that the right people would be in the right place, so in the end everything would come out the way God had ordained from the beginning. God never violates anyone's free will, but everything happens as He plans. God's providence in action.

Chapter 7
Types of Dreams

Spiritual dreams versus natural dreams dreaming is natural to all of us. It's a function that is common to every human being. Most of our dreams are the results of natural human function. Every Christian needs to be aware that sometimes, God uses this natural function in a supernatural way. Do you want to know if a dream is from God? When you dream, you see the dream in a natural state, but it often times reflects the spiritual realm. Usually dreams can be difficult to discern or interpret.

No doubt it's a very subjective experience, but most of us have had the feeling that some dreams are not like the rest. The images in the dreams lingers, and your emotions are affected, and the dreams stays with you. You feel that you just experienced a message from above a message that needs explanation. When we do receive a spiritual dream, it is usually one of the three types:

Warning dreams- this type is meant to warn us about some future attack from the enemy or some difficult times ahead. This could be a warning about a friend, spouse, or a child. These are given so that we might pray and intercede for the individual or the circumstance. Often times, the calamity is not decreed from above and through prayer the hardship can be avoided. An example in Genesis 20:1-18, Abimelech was warned not to sleep with Abraham's wife.

Confirmation dream- this dream simply confirms that which you believe to be true about a person or situation is in

63

fact true. This type of dream is used to give you emotional impetus to act on what you already know to be true. This is far from being unresponsive towards the dream. An example in Matthew 27:19, When Pilate's wife dream confirming that her husband should release Jesus from custody.

Prophetic dream -is a dream which reveals the future concerning yourself, another individual, etc. An example is Joseph's dream about his future in a place of honor and in high governmental service. Genesis 37:8

Spiritual dreams are God's sole prerogative, so we must always be ready when they do come. We need to quickly record them and then begin to pray for the interpretation. Spiritual dreams when heeded will keep us in the Will of God and remind us that we do indeed serve a God who knows us intimately and who takes the time to speak to His children individually.

IF
You can
Dream it,
You can
Do
it!

-Anonymous

Chapter 8
Five Ways to know if your Dreams are From God

1. Are your dreams Biblical?

All of us have dreams. The question is whether or not any of these dreams are the type of dreams that are sent to us from God to communicate to us.

In the book of Joel 2:28- And it shall come to pass afterward that I will pour out my Spirit upon all flesh and your sons and your daughters shall prophesy your old men shall dream dreams your young men shall see visions.

2. How can you tell if your dreams are from God and biblically based.

The Bible warns us about being deceived by different forms or spiritualism sorcery" including psychics ask yourself this question. Did the dream encourage me to do things that are contrary to the word of God? If it did, this dream is not of God. Any dreams that is contrary to the Word of God is not of God.

3. Is the dream revealing?

The reason that God sends dreams is that He is trying to reveal or communicate with you and not through normal means. In the Bible dreams always reveal something.

In the case of Jacob dream of the stairway to heaven. It revealed an aspect of God that Jacob had never understood before. Apostle Paul dream revealed that he was to go to Macedonia instead of another city.

The word reveal mean to make that which was previously unknown or of secret information known to others.

66

4. Does the dream remain in your memory?

Dreams from God are remembered, they stay with us and trouble our spirits. Our spirits ponder the realization that there is something there that is different from the norm. It's supernatural, it's out of the ordinary, King Nebuchadnezzar in the book of Daniel 2:3, had a dream.

The king had Daniel to interpret the dream for him because it troubled his spirit. A dream from God is different from a normal dream.

5. Did it come to pass?

The final proof of a dream from God is the results. Did it come to pass, for at that appointed time dreams from God will come to pass. Joseph dream came to pass, and sometimes we have to wait on the fulfillment of the dream because any God-given dream will come to pass!

YOU'LL KNOW WHEN
YOU'RE
DREAMING
BECAUSE
DREAMING
ALTERS YOUR
LIFE!

-T. Green

Chapter 9
Summary of Joseph's Life

Joseph is the most complete type of Christ images in the entire Bible. Notice the amazing similarities between Jesus and Joseph:

- Both were beloved by their fathers **(Genesis 37:3; Matthew 3:17)**
- Both regarded themselves as shepherds **(Genesis 37:2; John 10:11-14)**
- Both were sent to their brethren by their fathers **(Genesis 37:13-14; Luke 20:13)**
- Both were hated by their brethren without cause **(Genesis 37:4,5,8; John 1:11, 7:5, 15:25)**
- Both were plotted against by their brethren **(Genesis 37:20; John 11:35)**
- Both were severely tempted **(Genesis 39:7, Matthew 4:1)**
- Both were taken to Egypt **(Genesis 37:26, Matthew 2:14-15)**
- Both were stripped of their robes **(Genesis 37:23; John 19: 23-24)**
- Both were sold for the price of a slave **(Genesis 37:28; Matthew 26:15)**
- Both were bound **(Genesis 39:20; Matthew 27:2)**

- Both remained silent and offered no defense **(Genesis 39:20; Isaiah 53:7)**
- Both were falsely accused **(Genesis 39:16-18; Matthew 26:59-60)**
- Both experienced God's presence through everything **(Genesis 39:2, 21, 23; John 16:32)**
- Both were respected by their jailor **(Genesis 39:21; Luke 23:47)**
- Both were placed with two prisoners, one of which was later lost and the other saved **(Genesis 40:2-3, 21-22; L**
- **uke 23:32)**
- Both were around 30 when their ministry began **(Genesis 41:46; Luke 3:23)**
- Both were highly exalted after their suffering **(Genesis 41:41; Philippians 2:9-11)**
- Both were lost to their brother for a while **(Genesis 42:7-8; Romans 10:1-3, 11:7-8)**
- Both forgave and restored their repentant brothers **(Genesis 45:1-15; Revelation 1:7)**

   The Meaning of Joseph – "God adds".

- He was the eleventh son of Jacob, and the eldest of two sons borne by Rachel **(Genesis 30:24)**. Joseph's life can be divided into five phases.

Joseph the beloved son of Jacob

Genesis 37:1-4

- Joseph was seventeen years old. He was a shepherd.

- He did not participate in his brothers' misconducts. In fact, he brought the reports of their mischief to his father, Jacob.

- He was the favorite son of Jacob. Jacob loved him more than all his brothers. Jacob made a coat of many colors for him.

- His brothers hated him for this reason and could not even speak to him kindly.

- Joseph was rather naive to tell his dreams to his brothers because he told them of his future supremacy, and his brothers' submission to him. This intensified their hatred towards him.

- So, when the opportunity came at Dothan, they planned to kill him. But Rueben tried to rescue him by persuading them not to kill him. His brothers sold him to the caravan of Ishmaelite going to Egypt.

- His life was changed in a moment, from being the beloved son to the slave in an unknown land- the land of Egypt.

- Joseph was sold to Potiphar, the captain of Pharaoh's guard.

71

Joseph at the Potiphar's House

Genesis 39:1-20

- He was a good administrator.

- He was a hardworking and faithful servant.

- He was fair and handsome. **(Genesis 39:6)**

- God was with him and made him prosper and successful.

- God blessed his master through him. **(Genesis 39:2)** (check out Blessed is the Man – Psalm 1 Bible Study)

- Potiphar, his master had entrusted him with the oversight for all his household affairs.

Temptation of Joseph:

- He was a young and handsome man. He was the head of the house. None would have known if he'd have given in to the temptation by Potiphar's wife.

- But, he had a healthy fear of God.

Genesis 39:9 – No one is greater in this house than I am. My master has withheld nothing from me except you, because you are his wife. How then could I do such a wicked thing and sin against God?"

- His temptation period was long.

- He tried to resist her as much as he could, but when time came, he had to flee from the place. (Also check out, How to overcome temptation and Temptation of Jesus Christ in the Wilderness)

- Due to the false accusation of Potiphar's wife, he was cast into prison. **(Genesis 39:20)**

- Once again, he paid the price for being righteous!

Joseph in the Prison

Genesis 39:20 – 41:37

- Once again, God was with him in all his trials.

- One may argue, why did God not rescue him from his troubles? But God's plan and purpose are higher than ours. We may see the immediate, but God sees at our future.

- Joseph continued to be faithful.

- The Lord again blessed him in all his work. The Jailer gave him charge of all the other prisoners.

- In prison, he helped the chief butler (cup-bearer) to restore his position in Pharaoh's office. But the cupbearer forgot his promise to mention about Joseph's innocence to the Pharaoh.

- After two years, when Pharaoh had two dreams, the cupbearer remembered Joseph and his skills to interpret dreams.

73

- When Joseph was brought to Pharaoh, he interpreted dreams about seven years of plenty followed by seven years of famine.

- He suggested the preparation for the famine by storing food during the good harvest years. (Also check out Jesus feeding the five thousand)

Joseph: The Chief Minister (Governor) of Egypt

Genesis 41:41-56

- The Pharaoh liked his proposal. And he made Joseph the Head of State to implement his plans for upcoming (or anticipated) famine.

- He was given an Egyptian name and was married to an Egyptian priest's daughter.

- He was 30 years old when the God-given dream was fulfilled. After 13 years of suffering and struggle, God made him the most influential person in all of the known world at that time.

- His wisdom and planning saved the lives of people from not only Egypt, but many other nations.

Joseph's Life: The Unusual Family Reunion

Genesis 42-50

- The famine brought all people from different nations to Egypt for help, including his brothers from Israel.

- They could not recognize him, but he knew them. He remembered the dream he had, when he was a young boy.

- Joseph, after testing them in different ways, made himself known to them. (Genesis 45:1-15)

- He forgave them and persuaded them to settle in Egypt with their father, Jacob during the time of famine.

- Joseph lived for 110 years. **(Genesis 50:26)**

Lessons Learned from the Life of Joseph:

- God's plans and purpose are greater and better than ours!

- God provides and blesses those who persevere to follow Him.

- Suffering to God's people is not always bad! God can use the most painful time of our life for His good.

- Joseph teaches us

- The value of self-control in the temptation of the youth.

- Patience and perseverance in the time of troubles.

- Honesty, and the value of a strong work ethics.

- Fear of God and Faithfulness to God.

DREAM JOURNAL

Be Determined...

...Dare To Dream!

Made in the USA
Middletown, DE
18 June 2017